# HUMBLE PIE
## Self Help Book for the Child in You

# BY MAJO
### ILLUSTRATED BY BARBARA PRUITT
### ENHANCED BY MATT LERAY

ISBN: 1496109570
ISBN 13: 9781496109576

Library of Congress Control Number: 2014904223
CreateSpace Independent Publishing Platform
North Charleston, South Carolina

In a little bakery shop on the corner of Rising and Dough Streets, there once lived a "Humble Pie." Humble had many friends because she was so kind and hardly ever did anything to make the other pastries sour toward her.

Why, just last week, Humble watched Mrs. Cherry Pie's seven little tarts so she could go to the Pie Cutter's Ball. What a job that was! The cherry tarts were very sticky and hard to handle, but Humble Pie didn't complain.

In fact, when Mrs. Cherry Pie came to pick the tarts up, Humble said, "Anytime! They were no bother at all." (Under her crust, she thought, "Never again! Why, those little tarts didn't give me a minute's peace.")

Humble was always polite and courteous. She made sure the freshest pastries got the front row in the showcase. Then, eager customers would see them first and want to take the goodies home to enjoy.

Humble Pie was always telling others how beautiful and "good-enough-to-eat" they looked. But when the cakes tried to compliment her, she was quick to point out her browned edges and lumpy shape.

5

"How do I look, Humble?" asked the lemon meringue pie.

"Delectable!" answered Humble. "But let me curl your topping a little more to make you look glamorous."

"What about me?" asked the lemon chiffon pie. "I'm prettier than she is."

"Now, now," Humble said with a sigh. "You mustn't be jealous. You're both beautiful."

"Yeah, but Lemon Chiffon will lose her shape quicker than I will!" snapped Lemon Meringue.

"Well, your top gets hard as a stale roll," replied Lemon Chiffon.

9

"Girls, girls, you're spoiling your looks with all this bickering. Now climb right up in front so everyone can see you. And remember, keep smiling!"

"Those two," muttered Humble. "If it weren't for me, they'd have been mush long ago. They're both so delicate, but what tempers they have underneath!"

"Hey, Apple, Blueberry, and Peach, where are you," shouted Humble. "Oh, there you are. Come along, boys, or you'll be late. You know you shouldn't play in the kitchen. The heat will make you soggy. Now, climb into the case before you get stale."

"Oh my, where is Coconut? Still sleeping, I'll bet. That pie will be the death of me. He's always late, and so slow moving."

Poor Humble Pie! She really had her work cut out for her, keeping the other pies and pastries fresh and ready to eat.

She hardly ever had time for herself. Besides, it made her happy to help others…Or did it?

Sometimes, late at night, when the other pies were tucked in their warm ovens, she would cry to herself, "Why doesn't anybody appreciate all my hard work?"

"Everyone takes me for granted. 'Humble do this, Humble do that. Oh, Humble, you're so good.' If I'm so good, why don't they give me an award or something? Don't they know I have feelings, too? Under this lumpy crust, there's a heart that needs to be loved for who I am and not for what I do."

But how could they know? After all, they weren't pie readers, and Humble never told them how she really felt.

One day, a new pastry came to the little shop on Rising and Dough Streets.

13

It was called "Heavenly Cake." Heavenly was so handsome and strong looking that all of the other pastries got gooey just at the mention of his name. They looked to Heavenly for advice now.

Humble Pie felt abandoned. It was like being left on the back shelf.

"Poor me," cried Humble. "Nobody likes me. I'm worthless. I wish I would just fall off this shelf and PLOP—that would be the end of me."

Heavenly Cake always seemed to be in the right place at the right time. He heard Humble's cry and said, "You're not as humble as I thought."

Humble Pie was surprised at Heavenly's intrusion.

"Go away," said Humble. "I don't need your advice."

"I think you do," said Heavenly Cake. "All of the times you helped others, I thought it was for their benefit. But now I see that it was for yours."

"What do you mean?" snapped Humble Pie. "Why, I never do anything for myself. I always take care of others. Look at the thanks I get… a back-row seat with the crumb buns."

"If you were really a humble pie, you wouldn't need any thanks," said Heavenly Cake.

"But look at all the good things I do," said Humble.

"Humble," said Heavenly, "it doesn't matter how much you do. It only matters where your heart is when you are doing it. If you help others only for the praise you will receive, what good is there in that?"

"But I do feel happy when I help others," said Humble. "Is that bad?"

"No, no," said Heavenly Cake. "But why don't you help yourself?"

19

"I am a lost cause," said Humble Pie. "I can't do anything right. I am too lumpy. My edges are too brown, and now that I'm getting older, they're even beginning to crumble."

"I don't see any lumps," said Heavenly, "and I like brown, crumbly crust."

"You do?" exclaimed Humble. "I didn't think anybody would like the way I look."

"You spend too much time looking at your weaknesses," said Heavenly. "Why, you're so round and fully packed that you're just bursting with sweetness. And oh, your aroma…it makes my mouth water!"

"You're just kidding me," said Humble. "I know that's not true."

"Sure, it is. Frequently, I've seen customers come in, point to you, and say, 'I'll take that one,'" Heavenly said.

"You would always push another ahead of you and say, 'Take her, she's better.' But they wanted you.

"Why do you suppose they wanted you?" probed Heavenly. "Do you think it was because you're too lumpy or too brown or too crumbly? Nah, it's because you made their eyes widen and their lips smack with thoughts of your goodness."

"REALLY?" exclaimed Humble.

"Really," replied Heavenly.

"You mean I'm that good and I don't have to do anything but just be myself?" asked Humble.

"All you have to do is believe in yourself," said Heavenly. "Just keep telling yourself, 'I'm beautiful and I'm good enough to eat.'"

"But isn't that being proud?" asked Humble sheepishly. "I don't like proud, boastful pies. They make my edges curl and my juices curdle."

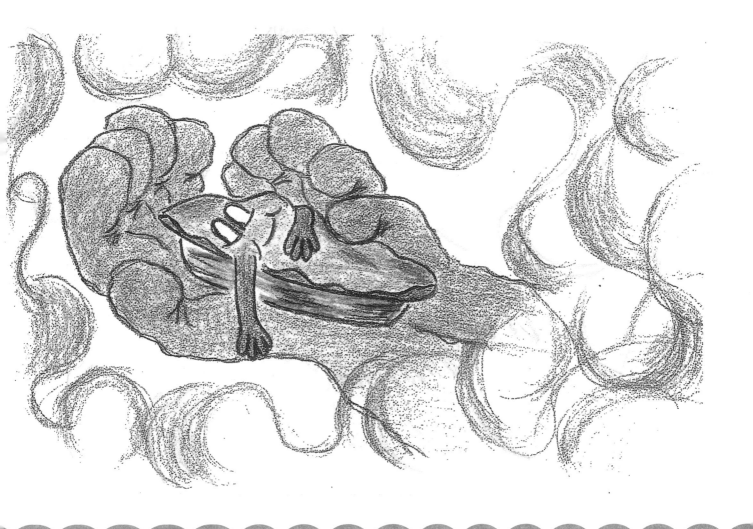

"Humble, when you were created and formed by the Master Chef, you were given many gifts," said Heavenly Cake. "Your pastry was filled to overflowing, and your edges were hand fluted just the right way.

"Maybe you are not as delicate as the chiffons or as beautiful as the lemon meringues, but you have special qualities that belong to only you. If you never used them or told others about them, Chef would feel very hurt—as if his work was in vain. Why do you suppose Chef creates so many different varieties?" asked Heavenly.

"Because chefs like to bake," Humble said, giggling.

"Perhaps. But I think it is because everyone has his or her own special tastes. Besides, no two pastries are exactly alike," said Heavenly Cake.

"The Master Chef made you, and you must be proud of yourself just the way you are," said Heavenly. "As a matter of fact, to be humble is to know what your special gifts are. Then you can thank the Master Chef for those gifts and not be ashamed or embarrassed to share them with others."

"But that's so hard. I don't know if I can do it," said Humble.

"You can," said Heavenly. "All you have to do is believe. Now, dust yourself off with some flour, climb into the showcase, and pick a front-row spot. No sitting in the back. Put your freshest, warmest smile on, and be yourself."

"Do you believe you are special?" asked Heavenly. "Do you believe you are one of a kind? Do you believe you're beautiful? Do you believe there is no pie as wonderful as you are?"

"I believe!" said Humble Pie,
"I believe... I believe..... I BELIEVE!!!"

## Author Biography

Majo is a wife, mother, grandmother, writer and entrepreneur who promotes positive thinking, and achieving a high quality of life. While raising her family, she began her career as a corporate consultant, training employees in team building, sales and diversity. She also earned a real estate license, wrote a column called "The Family Hour" for a Philadelphia area newspaper and modeled in print and television. She founded three businesses to foster personal accountability, successful parenting and improving the prevalent cultural mindset regarding women in advertising.

Of all her many accomplishments, Majo is most proud of being the mother of her eight children and the grandmother of many. Majo is a beautiful, energetic and determined entrepreneur. "Humble Pie" is the first book in a six book series. It has taken her 30 years and many, many rejection letters to achieve this goal. The saying "It's never too late" and Bob Dylan's quote "He whose not busy being born, is busy dying" motivate Majo to keep growing.

Majo is married and lives in Smithville, NJ.

Contact Majo at her website: majo the author.com or email her at mjbgd@aol.com